Mushrooming without fear

Alexander Schwab

It is easy to do without silver and gold
and your toga and cloak
but it is difficult to give up mushrooms.

Martial, Roman poet (AD 40 – 102)
Epigrams, Book 13, Number 48

Mushrooming without fear

Alexander Schwab

Consultants Monika Lehmann and Roy Mantle

First published by Merlin Unwin Books Ltd (Ludlow UK) in 2006

Merlin Unwin Books
Palmers House
7 Corve Street
Ludlow
Shropshire SY8 1DB
UK
www.merlinunwin.co.uk

ISBN 1 873674 88 0
ISBN 978 1 873674 88 8

Picture credits:
Frank Moser: cep page 40, middle picture cep page 42, orange birch bolete, page 68
Thomas Beer: larch boletes bottom right and middle right, page 57
Niels Sloth (www.biopix.dk): pestle shaped puffball, page 90

Design and production by Kurt Wüst
Printed and bound by Star Standard Industries (PTE) Ltd

Contents

Mushrooming without fear

It's safe, easy and fun

Follow this guide and you can enjoy picking and eating delicious mushrooms untrammelled by fear and doubt. In order to enjoy a home-made gourmet mushroom dinner you do not really need to know what *basidia or hyphae* are. Nor do you need to know how to identify dozens of tasteless or poisonous mushrooms which you wouldn't want to eat in the first place.

Some people find it really difficult not to pick everything they spot. It might be edible, they think. They're encouraged in this attitude by encyclopaedic mushroom identification books displaying a bewildering multitude of beautiful mushrooms. This induces indiscriminate mushroom hunting of the 'pick first, ask questions later' variety, which is the wrong approach. Back home, attempts to identify the edible ones with the help of a conventional mushroom identification book invariably fail because of the complexity of the task.

It is tempting to pick every beautiful mushroom one comes across. But indiscriminate mushroom hunting is not only dangerous, it makes a nonsense of conservation.

You wouldn't buy a soggy, wormy, half rotten mushroom in the supermarket. So why pick it in the wood? Quality is what the discerning mushroom hunter is after.

Even advanced mushroom pickers often face too many uncertainties. The same mushroom looks different in the various stages of its development and different again when conditions are, for example, very wet or very dry. There are no end of edible mushrooms. Twenty-odd of these are of serious culinary interest, of which about a dozen are outstanding. Quality, not quantity, is what you are after. By good luck, the quality mushrooms are also among the most easily identifiable mushrooms and some of these are among the most frequently encountered.

Conventional mushroom guides always include warnings against look-alike poisonous species. This simply adds to the uncertainty, as these warning comparisons introduce new elements into an already confusing situation. With the safe method explained in this book, you will be able to identify the best mushrooms positively by their unique and unmistakeable features.

The fly agaric is the most well-known species. For gnomes, pixies, fairies and other such folk it is safe. For us common mortals it is poisonous! Do not believe any old wives' tales regarding the identification of poisonous mushrooms. Stick to the safe method in order to identify the best edible mushrooms.

Your part in the safe method is:

1. Be disciplined enough to leave alone most mushrooms you pass
2. Look closely at what you see before you, not at what you wish was there
3. Stick to the rules and tick off every stage in the mushroom identification process

Why is the safe method, safe? If you follow the safe method to the letter, you'll automatically steer clear of deadly mushrooms or mushrooms causing permanent damage. Always remember that modern medicine can't do anything to save your life if you eat the wrong mushroom.

In the families of mushrooms presented and recommended here, there is not one deadly mushroom.

This is the reason why the field mushroom is not in this guide.

The field mushroom belongs to the group of mushrooms with gills, and especially when young, the field mushroom can be confused with some deadly species. The safe method therefore asks you to ignore all mushrooms with gills because it is within the gilled group that all the seriously poisonous and deadly mushrooms are found. If you're absolutely sure about the field mushroom, then pick it by all means. But unless you are 100 per cent certain, hunt for field mushrooms and other species with gills in the supermarket only.

Within the recommended groups you will find some slightly poisonous mushrooms but these happen to be so bitter, hot-tasting or strong-smelling that nobody sane would eat them anyway should they find their way into a meal (which they won't if you follow the safe method). Poisonous mushrooms in the recommended groups cause gastro-intestinal trouble of varying intensity. In other words: tummy ache. Nevertheless there is absolutely no reason for complacency: a harmless tummy ache together with an existing medical condition can be dangerous.

Mushrooming without fear focuses exclusively on identifying safe mushrooms with a culinary angle. The handling, storage and cooking of mushrooms is treated in greater depth on the website, together with further details of mushroom foraging.

www.mushrooming.co.uk

How to use this guide

1. Read the entire book **twice** in order to understand the approach

2. Study the 'Gills', 'Tubes', 'Spines' and 'Ridges' sections until you're confident you can correctly distinguish these features; then you're ready for a foray

3. Take the field identification card with you and pick only those mushrooms you're reasonably sure are on the ID card

4. Double-check at home by going through the full identification process step-by-step

The size of mushrooms

The size of mushrooms varies enormously, so any measurements given in this book are only a rough average. Don't be put off if you see an exception. The size can vary disproportionately due to weather conditions: if it is very dry, the mushrooms will be smaller than average. The other great variable is the growing medium. Don't be surprised if, on Forestry Commission land, for example, you find surprisingly large mushrooms growing out of sawdust, or where woodchip has been laid at the edge of paths.

What is a mushroom?

A mushroom is a highly complex organism. Here are the essentials:

Fruitbody

The technical term for what is colloquially called the 'mushroom' is the 'fruitbody'. Mycologically speaking, the real mushroom is the mycelium which is a fine structure of filaments on or in the forest soil. What we see as mushrooms (the fruitbody) are like the apples on an apple tree.

Cap

The caps of mushrooms have many different forms but what we're interested in is what is under the cap. Under the cap you'll find either...

Gills

Tubes

Spines

Ridges

Gills, tubes, spines and ridges produce, contain and release the spores. Wind and rain disperse the spores. Given the right conditions new mycelia and mushrooms form from the spores.

Stalk

Mycelium

The mycelium

This is a close-up of about 4 mm of the mycelium above, as seen under a microscope. When conditions are right, the mycelium forms a fruitbody, pushing the mushroom up in order to disperse the spores or to wait for you to come along and pick it.

Rule number 1

Never, never take a mushroom with gills!!!

Gills

Identifying gills is the first and most important step. You must be sure that you're able to identify gills. Caps of gilled mushrooms come in many different shapes. Gills are the radiating blades on the underside of the cap. They fan out in a distinctly regular way. Gills have precise forms and come in many colours. Some of them are brittle some of them are soft. They can be rubbed off or separated from the underside of the cap quite easily. Gills are always attached to the stem or to the cap in a uniform way.

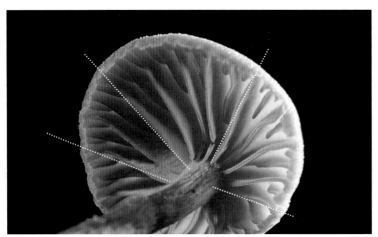

In perfect conditions the distinctly regular way in which the gills fan out is clearly visible.

Weather-beaten or old gills might be damaged or broken but on closer inspection their regularity will become apparent. Damage or no damage: either way they look as if drawn with a ruler.

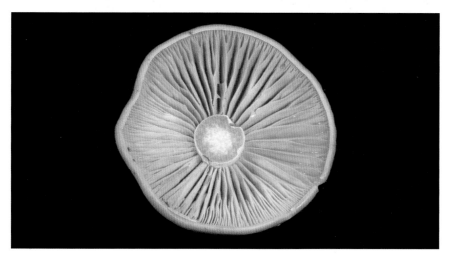

In their regular way, gills differ in spacing and formation.
For example:

Gills can fork once or more.

Gills can be mixed: long and short gills.

Gills can be crowded.

Gills can be distant.

Gills are always uniformly attached to the cap or the stem. They start radiating from the same height along the stem or the same line around the cap.

Rule number 2

Only take mushrooms with tubes, spines and ridges and the mavericks portrayed in this book

Tubes

Tubes are fine and tightly packed on the underside of the cap. The openings at the ends of the tubes are called pores.

Spines

Spines hang like stalactites from the cap.

Ridges

Ridges are cross-veined, irregular and don't form a distinct pattern. Ridges are not attached to the cap: they are part of the cap.

Remember Rule number 1

Never, never take a mushroom with gills!!!

Tubes

This is the underside of a cap with tubes. The tubes are fine and tightly packed and the openings at the end which are seen here are called pores. Tubes can be removed easily from the cap.

Pores form a regular pattern resembling a sponge.

This cross-section shows the tubes and the pores.

Tubes

Pores

Spines

Spines hang like stalactites from the cap.

Ridges

Ridges are on the underside of the cap and are part of it. They are not just attached to the cap or stem: they're part of them, which is why you can't rub them off or pull them off easily.

Ridges are cross-veined, irregular and they don't form a set, uniform pattern.

They are not attached to the stem in a distinct and regular way, as gills are: they are part of the stem.

The ridges are part of the stem. There is no distinct pattern in the way they grow out of the stem. Some ridges begin further up, some further down the stem. There is no regularity.

In contrast to gills and tubes, the section of a mushroom with ridges shows no typical features. Because of the irregular nature of ridges each section will look different whereas with tubes and gills you will find the same features each time.

How to pick mushrooms

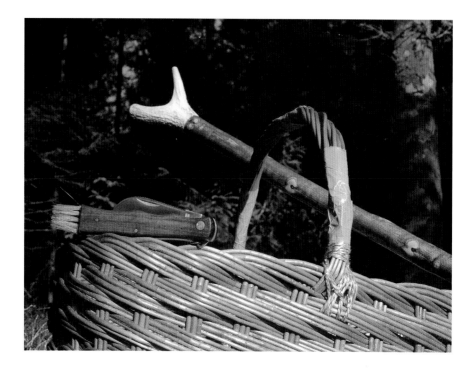

Rule number 1 says not to take anything with gills. This also means you **do not touch or cut every mushroom you spot** in order to check for gills.

In nine out of ten cases you can see whether a mushroom has gills or not without even touching it. Looking under the cap by kneeling down provides good exercise.

If you really can't see what's underneath a cap, break off just a little to see what's there. If you want to be absolutely safe, you could use surgical gloves or a paper handkerchief which you discard later.

If you have established that you have, say, a mushroom with tubes and it is in reasonable condition and it tallies with the field identification card – then, and only then, should you pick it.

Rules:

Rule number 1

Never, never take a mushroom with gills!!!

This is our life insurance.

Rule number 2

Only take mushrooms with tubes, spines and ridges and the mavericks portrayed in this book

This means thoroughly understanding the information on pages 18-27 of this book.

Rule number 3

Only eat mushrooms which you have clearly identified with ALL the positive ID marks

The mushrooms you take must be a certain size in order to show all the identification marks. In their baby stage, so to speak, some deadly and poisonous mushrooms are almost indistinguishable from harmless species.

Rule number 4

If a mushroom smells rotten, it is rotten and if it feels soggy, it is soggy

There are a surprising number of people who believe that somehow a half decomposed, soggy, smelly mushroom will improve on the way home. It never does. Only take mushrooms which are in mint condition, that is, the flesh is firm and there are hardly any worms.

Rule number 5

Never, never eat wild mushrooms raw

The reasons for this are manifold but, to state the obvious, some areas in some woods are dog-ridden.

Rule number 6

Look before you cut

Always cut mushrooms, do not pull them out. You don't chop down an apple tree to pick the apples. Cut just above the ground and cover the remaining stem with a little mud or dead leaves. Whether this is of any conservational value is disputed but it does no harm. My recommendation is to cut and cover. More about this on the website: www.mushrooming.co.uk

Picked mushrooms want to breathe. Do not suffocate them in plastic bags. Use a wicker or rattan basket or a linen bag. If possible use a proper mushroom knife with an integrated brush for cleaning. As the first cleaning of the mushroom should be done in the woods, the brush is very useful. However, any knife will do, as long as the blade can be folded into the knife handle, for safety. Common sense is your best adviser but be aware of any likelihood of ticks where you go mushrooming.
More on safety on the website
www.mushrooming.co.uk

You might want a stick. It can be any kind of stick and you will find it helpful on the slopes. But you will also find it useful for pushing aside the grass and ferns, affording you a better look at the ground. Different mushrooms can be put together in your wicker basket . Better still, have a few paper bags in the basket; one paper bag (breathable) for each species. Putting, say, all trumpet chanterelles in the same bag helps you to spot the odd one out which you have inadvertently cut while not fully concentrating (see page 78).

Rule number 7

Mushrooms want to breathe:
Do not suffocate them in plastic bags

Either in the woods or at home.

Rule number 8

If in doubt, leave it

Now you're ready for a foray.

Positively identifying mushrooms

Always remember

Rule number 1

    Never, never take a mushroom with gills!!!

Rule number 2

    Only take mushrooms with tubes, spines and ridges and
the mavericks portrayed in this book

Rule number 3

    Only eat mushrooms which you have clearly identified
with ALL the positive ID marks

Rule number 4

    If a mushroom smells rotten, it is rotten and if it feels
soggy, it is soggy

Rule number 5

    Never, never eat wild mushrooms raw

Rule number 6

    Look before you cut

Rule number 7

    Mushrooms want to breathe. Do not suffocate them in
plastic bags

Rule number 8

    If in doubt, leave it

Mushrooms with tubes

Cep or Penny Bun Bolete
Boletus edulis

The cep is the king of mushrooms. Some truffles are rarer, pricier and confined to relatively small areas in France and Southern Europe. The cep on the other hand reigns supreme everywhere. Ceps can be found in the same location year after year. They can disappear in certain areas for a couple of years only to return spectacularly in masses. Some people gather only ceps which is understandable because of their beauty, taste and the thrill of finding them on the same spot time after time. Ceps vary greatly in general appearance, colour and size. The size of the little fellow in the foreground of the picture above is about 5cm in height whereas the giant is about 35cm in height.

If conditions are right (starting off with a nice wet and humid spring or early summer) you should begin to look for ceps as early as the beginning of July. July and August are the months of the summer ceps.

White network

White network

These are summer ceps. However all ceps, summer or autumn, show a fine white network on the top of the stem right underneath the tubes.

A classic autumn cep,
the king of mushrooms.

This is the key ID mark. The white net-pattern must be visible! All ceps, regardless of their time of emerging or stage of their development, have a fine white net-pattern at the top of their stalk.

This is what a cep ideally looks like when cut. Not a single worm has even looked at this beauty. The tubes and the flesh do not change colour when cut or touched.

Cep tubes are off-white and firm when young. Later they turn yellow-olive and are less firm. In maturity the tubes are olive. Tubes of mature ceps are soft as a sponge and the tubes of old ones are soggy and often like those of the big fellow on page 38. This does not always mean that the inside of old ceps is rotten but more often than not , it is.

Cep stalks vary greatly in appearance. These specimens clearly show the white net-pattern all over the stalk.

Nevertheless, it is that top section of the stalk just below the cap where it matters: there the white network must be clearly visible.

Positive ID Checklist
Cep or Penny Bun Bolete

- [ ] Tubes, pores and flesh do not change colour when cut or bruised
- [ ] Tubes are off-white, cream, yellow-olive or olive
- [ ] Pores do not show any pink tinge
- [ ] White network on top of stem
- [ ] Cap matches the colour bar range (above)

Avg. size across cap: 130mm

Appearance: July to November

Habitat: Underneath beech, oak, birch and pine trees.

Tip: Where you find one cep, you'll often find others in the vicinity.

Culinary rating: 10 out of 10.

'Edulis' means 'edible'.

Red Cracked Bolete

Xerocomus chrysenteron

The red cracked bolete is probably the most common of all mushrooms with tubes. Its name describes its key identification feature perfectly. As the mushroom matures, the cracks become more prominent. Some people love eating the red cracked bolete, others quite like it and there are a few who don't take to it at all. The reason is its distinct fruity smell. In any case the red cracked bolete should only be picked as long as the pores are bright yellow and firm. The ideal size of the cap is about 2 to 3cm across. Anything larger will make your dish all slimy.

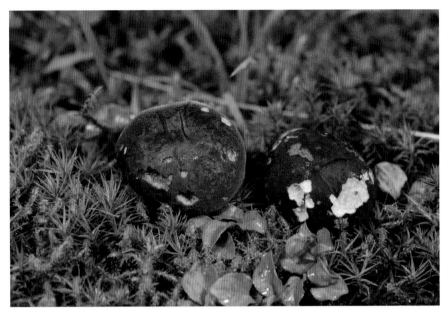

The colour of the cap ranges from a velvety dark brown to a light brown.

Stems vary in colour from yellow, to yellow with a little red to yellow flushed with red. Note the bright yellow pores. The stem and the pores bruise blue. The intensity of the blueing varies. See picture opposite page, far left.

This specimen is too old for the kitchen. The pores have lost their brightness. The dull yellow signals that its no good anymore. When the pores are this colour, the mushroom feels soft-to-soggy.

This is the perfect specimen. It has bright, firm golden-yellow pores and a nice firm cap about 3 cm across.

The caps are invariably cracked or lightly damaged. The typical identification mark of the red cracked bolete is the red showing through the cracks or the eaten-away patches.

When cut, the white-to-bright-yellow flesh turns blue. This can be very light blue and confined to certain patches.

Positive ID Checklist
Red Cracked Bolete

- ☐ **Yellow tubes**
- ☐ **Yellow pores bruise blue (varying intensity)**
- ☐ **Flesh bruises blue (varying intensity)**
- ☐ **Cracks and damaged patches in cap show a distinct red tinge**
- ☐ **Cap matches the colour bar (above)**

Avg. size across cap:	50mm
Appearance:	June to November
Habitat:	Seems to feel at home everywhere
Tip:	Take only small specimens
	(ie cap no wider than 30mm across)
Culinary rating:	Small specimens 7 out of 10

Chrysenteron means 'with golden-yellow flesh'.

Dotted Stemmed Bolete

Boletus erythrophus

In terms of culinary value and aesthetic appeal, the dotted stemmed bolete is on a par with the cep. It appears as early as August and, given favourable conditions, can be found well into November. What's more, there can be bumper years. Cooking the dotted stemmed bolete turns the sauce dark, which doesn't matter. If however you want to avoid a dark sauce, blanch the ready-to-cook pieces and discard the water.

There is no typical shape for the dotted stemmed bolete. Likewise the colour of its velvety cap ranges from a leathery brown yellow to deep dark brown. The pore colour is light to deep orange-red.

When you think you have found a dotted stemmed bolete, do not cut it open right away. Look at it from the outside first.

The stalk when cut turns blue immediately. The orange-red pores bruise blue. The flesh is yellow.

When cut , the dotted stemmed bolete starts blueing immediately (left). The deep blue fades out after a couple of minutes (right).

Flesh and tubes instantly turn blue after cutting. Nevertheless there is enough time to see that flesh and tubes are at first yellow before blueing.

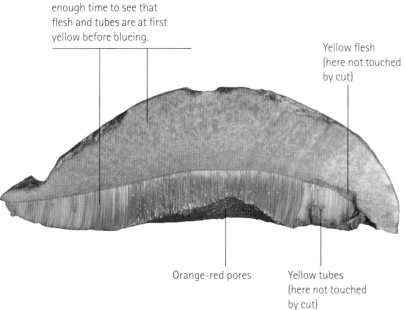

Yellow flesh
(here not touched
by cut)

Orange-red pores

Yellow tubes
(here not touched
by cut)

Detail of stem which also bruises blue. Note the dot pattern.

The key identification mark is the red dots on the stem. The dots must be clearly visible.

Dot pattern on stem

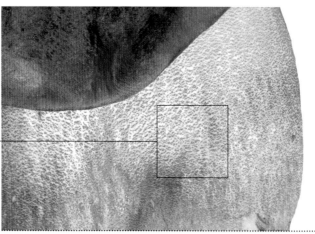

Some dots might have been eaten away. For safe identification large patches of dots must be clearly visible.

Positive ID Checklist
Dotted Stemmed Bolete

- ☐ **Orange-red pores**
- ☐ **Pores bruise blue**
- ☐ **Yellow tubes**
- ☐ **Tubes bruise blue**
- ☐ **Yellow flesh**
- ☐ **Flesh (stalk and cap) instantly turns blue when cut**
- ☐ **Dotted stem**
- ☐ **Cap colour matches colour bar (above)**

Avg. size across cap:	100mm
Appearance:	August to November
Habitat:	Seems to feel at home everywhere. Likes acidic soil
Tip:	If you find one you'll almost always find several in the vicinity
Culinary rating:	10 out of 10

Erythropus means 'red foot'

Larch Bolete
Suillus grevillei

It is as if pure gold has grown out of the ground – and where there is one nugget, there are others. It's very rare to find a single larch bolete. More often than not larch boletes form a fairy ring. Always found near larch trees, this beautiful and delicious mushroom is covered with a yellow veil when young (above left). As the maturing mushroom grows, the veil breaks, leaving a transient ring on the stalk (above, centre and right). Always peel the cap of the larch bolete on the spot because otherwise it will make your basket and later your recipe all slimy. In wet conditions, the cap of the larch bolete is always slimy.

The veil still covers
the cap in a 'baby'
larch bolete.

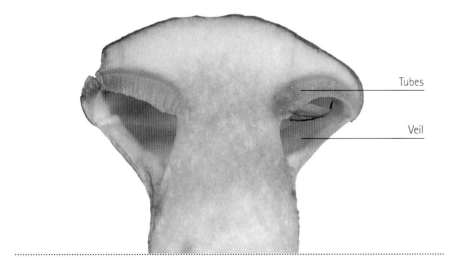

Tubes

Veil

The tubes must
be clearly visible
when you view a
cross-section.

Tubes | Solid stem | Faint lilac colouring | Veil

As the mushroom grows, the veil breaks. This picture (right) shows a larch bolete shortly after the breaking of the veil. The ring is transient (ie it often drops off) but even in the mature larch bolete you can always see a mark where the ring has been.

Above the ring marks: net pattern (can be very faint). Below the ring marks: mature specimens show distinct reddish-rusty streaks on the yellow stem.

If a larch tree is nearby and you see several gold nuggets, they are bound to be larch boletes. The beautifully golden (and slimy when wet) caps are the key sign. Positive identification however requires ticking off all of the identification marks.

Positive ID Checklist
Larch Bolete

- [ ] **Yellow tubes**
- [ ] **Solid stem**
- [ ] **Bright orange-yellow or golden-yellow sticky cap (slimy when wet). You have already checked all of the above in the wood with the field ID card.**
- [ ] **Flesh in cap flushes lilac (faint)**
- [ ] **Found near larch trees**
- [ ] **Other specimens found in the vicinity**
- [ ] **Young: tubes covered with a veil**
- [ ] **Intermediate stage: ring visible, faint net-pattern above ring zone**
- [ ] **Mature: ring zone still visible, faint network above ring zone**
- [ ] **Cap colour matches cap colour bar (above)**

Avg. size across cap:	70mm
Appearance:	June to October
Habitat:	Always near larch
Tip:	Always remove the cap skin
Culinary rating:	9 out of 10

'Grevillei' refers to the Scottish mycologist R.K. Greville

Bay Bolete

Xerocomus badius

The bay bolete is an excellent mushroom and by good luck, it is also very common. The main bay bolete months are September and October but it can be found as early as June. If you find one, there are bound to be others nearby.

Yellow pores:

This is the stage when the bay bolete is at its best. If the pores turn dirty yellow or green (see opposite page, top) the mushroom is past its culinary best. Take only specimens which have yellow or dirty-yellow pores.

Downwards-streaked stem:

The background colour of the stalk is yellow-brown and is vertically frosted with brown streaks. The general appearance of the stalk ranges from light to dark brown but the vertical streaks will always be visible.

The yellow pores bruise green-blue.

The change in colour of the pores to green-blue varies in intensity. Here it's quite extreme.

The young bay bolete has pale yellow tubes which then turn to yellow, olive-yellow and dirty olive-yellow as the mushroom matures. Whatever the stage, the tubes and the flesh bruise blue.

The intensity of the colouring varies but pores, tubes and flesh will always bruise green-blue.

This is what the ideal bay bolete looks like: yellow pores and tubes, white to white-yellow flesh, without a trace of a worm.

Not as good: but if you discard the soft pores and cut away the wormy parts, it will still be excellent.

The colour of the cap will always be 'bay' (chestnut brown) but bay has a considerable range.

When wet, the cap will be slightly slimy and this will intensify the colour of the cap.

When dry, the colour of the cap will be duller.

Positive ID Checklist
Bay Bolete

- ☐ **Yellow tubes**
- ☐ **Yellow pores bruise green-blue**
- ☐ **Tubes and flesh bruise blue**
- ☐ **Stem is vertically frosted with brown streaks**
- ☐ **There is no net-pattern of any description on the stem**
- ☐ **Cap colour matches cap colour bar (above)**

Avg. size across cap:	90mm
Appearance:	June to November
Habitat:	Prefers coniferous woods
Tip:	Remove soft tubes
Culinary rating:	10 out of 10

Badius means 'beautifully brown'

Birch Bolete

Leccinum scabrum

The birch bolete is the most common of the 'rough stalks'. Rough stalks are mushrooms with a scaly stem. The birch bolete and its cousin, the orange birch bolete, are the most common rough stalks. Birch woods or groups of birch trees are the places to look for them. The birch bolete and the orange birch bolete have numerous relatives, all of which have a black or brown scaly stalk. They are all edible but it is recommended to stick to the two species presented here.

Tubes off-white

Pores off-white

Pores bruise brownish

Stalk covered with black scales

Close-up of stalk, showing black scales.

Pores and tubes change from off-white to a grey-white colour as the mushroom matures. As a rule, you should only pick the birch bolete if it is firm and the pores are off-white.

Occasionally larger specimens are still nice and firm especially when conditions have been very dry.

These are the perfect birch boletes: a feast for the eyes and delicious to eat.

The orange birch bolete, *Leccinum versipelle*, is a beautiful mushroom. Its key identification mark is the stem covered with black scales, and of course the orange cap. When cut, the flesh turns faintly blue at the stalk base, displays traces of wine red and finally turns and stays grey. This colour combination doesn't look especially appetising but be assured the orange birch bolete is delicious.

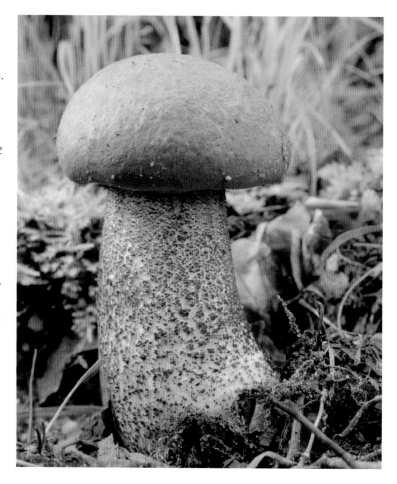

Positive ID Checklist
Birch Bolete

- ☐ **Pores off-white**
- ☐ **Pores bruise brownish**
- ☐ **Stalk with small black scales**
- ☐ **Cap colour matches cap colour bar (above)**

Avg. size across cap:	90mm
Appearance:	August to November
Habitat:	Birch woods, groups of birch, individual birch
Tip:	Discard stem and tubes of larger specimens
Culinary rating:	9 out of 10

Scabrum means 'rough'

Always remember

Rule number 1

 Never, never take a mushroom with gills!!!

Rule number 2

 Only take mushrooms with tubes, spines and ridges and the mavericks portrayed in this book

Rule number 3

 Only eat mushrooms which you have clearly identified with ALL the positive ID marks

Rule number 4

 If a mushroom smells rotten, it is rotten and if it feels soggy, it is soggy

Rule number 5

 Never, never eat wild mushrooms raw

Rule number 6

 Look before you cut

Rule number 7

 Mushrooms want to breathe. Do not suffocate them in plastic bags

Rule number 8

 If in doubt, leave it

Mushrooms with ridges

Chanterelle
Cantharellus cibarius

The chanterelle is not surprisingly the most popular mushroom.
It is delicious and very common. As it is imported throughout the year,
the supermarket is a good place to familiarize yourself with the
chanterelle. There is, however, nothing like the chanterelle you find
yourself. Refrain from picking tiny chanterelles, that is, little yellow
buttons which hardly show the identification marks. At some time
you'll come across one lonely chanterelle standing there in the middle
of nowhere for no particular reason at all. Leave it.

The classic colour of the chanterelle is egg-yolk yellow which, however, can vary from light yellow or yellow-orange to yellow-ochre. The chanterelle does not change colour when bruised. The entire mushroom is of the same colour.

Young chanterelles have a flat cap with a slightly out-rolled margin. Do not pick any chanterelles smaller than 3 cm high.

The more mature the chanterelle, the more funnel-shaped it becomes.

The stalk is solid. The whitish to yellowish flesh does not change colour when bruised or cut.

Whether young or mature, the chanterelle's ridges must be clearly visible.

Some mature forms can look highly irregular but on closer inspection, the funnel shape will still be there.

Positive ID Checklist
Chanterelle

- ☐ **Young specimen: Flat cap, slightly out-rolled margin**
- ☐ **Mature specimen: Funnel-shaped**
- ☐ **Solid stem**
- ☐ **Found in groups**
- ☐ **Ridges must be clearly visible**
- ☐ **Colour matches cap colour bar range (above)**

Avg. size across cap:	50mm
Appearance:	July to October
Habitat:	In woods with beech, oak, pine and birch
Tip:	Watch for mossy patches with little plant cover
Culinary rating:	10 out of 10. See page 115

Cibarius means 'belonging to food'

Trumpet Chanterelle
Cantharellus tubaeformis

In comparison to the attractively-coloured chanterelle, the trumpet chanterelle (also known as the autumn chanterelle, and winter chanterelle) looks modest. On closer inspection, however, it is just as beautiful as the chanterelle. The trumpet chanterelle pops up over-night so quickly that you could watch it grow. It is an endearing mushroom not least because it tends to appear in great numbers and is frost-resistant.

A cluster of trumpet chanterelles.

Colour and shape vary according to age and weather conditions. Each individual trumpet chanterelle has more than one colour. The cap is brownish and has a hole in the centre. The ridges and the stalk range from brown-yellow to grey-yellow to grey-lilac.

The jagged edges here are due to frost.

The trumpet chanterelle has a hollow stem.

The advantage of having a paper bag for each species (see page 32) is seen here. You can spot the odd one out immediately.

Positive ID Checklist
Trumpet Chanterelle

- [ ] **Found in groups**
- [ ] **Brownish cap with hole in centre**
- [ ] **Hollow stem**
- [ ] **Ridges**
- [ ] **Cap colour matches colour bar (above)**

Avg. size across cap:	20–25mm
Appearance:	August to November
Habitat:	Deciduous and coniferous woods
Tip:	Mossy banks are a favourite habitat
Culinary rating:	9 out 10

Tubaeformis means 'trumpet-shaped'

Always remember

Rule number 1

    Never, never take a mushroom with gills!!!

Rule number 2

    Only take mushrooms with tubes, spines and ridges and the mavericks portrayed in this book

Rule number 3

    Only eat mushrooms which you have clearly identified with ALL the positive ID marks

Rule number 4

    If a mushroom smells rotten, it is rotten and if it feels soggy, it is soggy

Rule number 5

    Never, never eat wild mushrooms raw

Rule number 6

    Look before you cut

Rule number 7

    Mushrooms want to breathe. Do not suffocate them in plastic bags

Rule number 8

    If in doubt, leave it

Mushrooms with spines

Hedgehog Fungus
Hydnum repandum

There are other mushrooms with spines but the only one of real culinary interest is the hedgehog fungus. The hedgehog fungus is a great delicacy. It grows on the ground but never on trees.

The spines are the key identification marks of the hedgehog fungus. The flesh is matt white and colours in places to a yellow-brown or rusty yellow.

Some hedgehog fungi grow in a very irregular fashion, up to the size of two fists. Nevertheless, all hedgehog fungi have distinctive spines. The specimens here show the entire colour range of the cap. No other mushroom with spines has these colours.

Take only specimens where the spines are clearly visible. The hedgehog fungi pictured here are the perfect size for the kitchen. The cap size is 7–10 cm across.

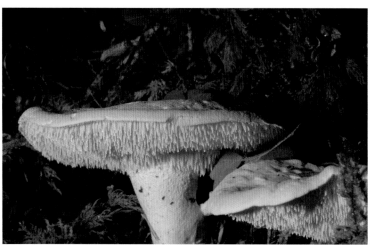

Positive ID Checklist
Hedgehog Fungus

- ☐ Spines
- ☐ Flesh matt white when freshly cut
- ☐ Flesh colours in places to yellow-brown or rusty yellow
- ☐ Found on ground but not on trees
- ☐ Cap colour matches colour bar (above)

Avg. size across cap: 60mm

Appearance: September to November

Tip: Avoid older specimens as they taste slightly bitter

Culinary rating: 10 out of 10

Repandum means 'bent upwards' (refers to the way the cap often reveals its underside)

Always remember

Rule number 1

> Never, never take a mushroom with gills!!!

Rule number 2

> Only take mushrooms with tubes, spines and ridges and the mavericks portrayed in this book

Rule number 3

> Only eat mushrooms which you have clearly identified with ALL the positive ID marks

Rule number 4

> If a mushroom smells rotten, it is rotten and if it feels soggy, it is soggy

Rule number 5

> Never, never eat wild mushrooms raw

Rule number 6

> Look before you cut

Rule number 7

> Mushrooms want to breathe. Do not suffocate them in plastic bags

Rule number 8

> If in doubt, leave it

Mavericks

Common Puffball

Lycoperdon perlatum

The common puffball is a curious little mushroom. One cluster of common puffballs might number merely four specimens; the next about forty. The common puffball is a welcome addition to any mix of mushrooms. Cooked on its own, it is not everyone's cup of tea because of its distinct taste. The giant puffball is another matter and as good a reason as you'll get for a dinner party.

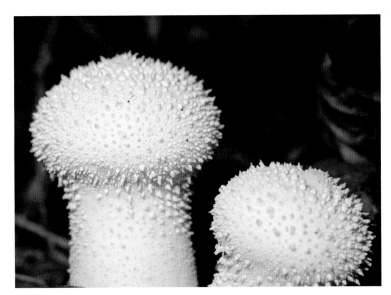

The conical spines are visible to the naked eye and leave an unmistakeable net-pattern when rubbed off. Only pick specimens on which the white conical spines are clearly visible. The common puffball has no unpleasant smell.

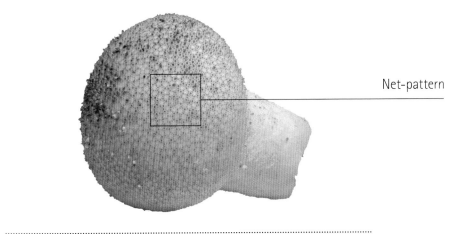

Net-pattern

These common puffballs are the perfect size (height 3–5 cm) and condition. When cut, the inside is all white and firm. Only when the flesh is uniformly white and firm, is the mushroom alright for use.

A variation of the common puffball is the pestle puffball. It too has spines but these are finer than those of the common puffball. It is pestle-shaped and it grows larger (height up to 20 cm) than the common puffball. It has no smell. If the flesh is uniformly white, and firm, it is good to eat.

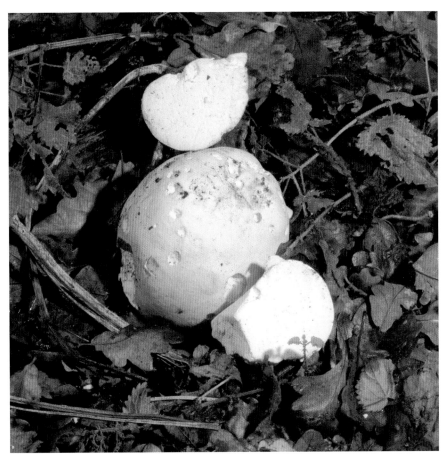

The big brother of the common puffball is the giant puffball. Giant means it can grow to one metre in diameter. From a distance it looks all white but it can have a light yellow or yellow-brown tinge. The surface is smooth and feels rather like suede. The small specimen cut in two in the picture is about the size of a fist. When cut open, the flesh must be white and firm. Only then is the giant puffball edible – and delicious at that.

Positive ID Checklist
Common Puffball

- [ ] Conical spines
- [ ] Flesh must be all-white
- [ ] Flesh must be firm
- [ ] Net-patterned when spines are rubbed off
- [ ] Colour white to off-white
- [ ] Found in groups
- [ ] No unpleasant smell
- [ ] Cap colour matches cap colour bar (above)

Avg. size across cap:	Size of a golf ball. Giant puffball 300mm
Appearance:	July to November
Habitat:	Seems to feel at home everywhere
Tip:	Giant puffballs always grow on the same spot
Culinary rating:	9 out of 10

Perlatum means 'widely-spread'

Horn of Plenty

Craterellus cornucopioides

The horn of plenty is a real challenge to the mushroom forager.
Growing low on the forest-floor, it is so well-camouflaged that you can
look at masses of them and not see any at all. If you spot one, there
will be more: proceed with the utmost care because they are easily
trampled. The horn of plenty is without a shadow of doubt one of the
most delicious mushrooms in the world. But it has its price. Cleaning
the horn of plenty can be quite a job but the reward is well worth the
effort. Besides, when everybody joins the cleaning party, it is fun.

The horn of plenty is a funnel, the outer side of which looks smooth but in fact is slightly wrinkled. The colour on the outer side is ash-grey, grey or pale grey with a bluish or lilac tint.

The inside of the funnel is brown, brown-grey, soot-grey or black. The surface is scurfy or flaky and the top is out-rolled. In older specimens the top is wavy and split.

The horn of plenty seen from above in dry conditions.

The horn of plenty seen from above in wet conditions.

The funnel shape and the out-rolled top are typical.

This looks a rather battered group of horn of plenty. Some of the tops have already split. Don't be put off – they still taste good.

Positive ID Checklist
Horn of Plenty

- ☐ **Found in groups**
- ☐ **Funnel shaped**
- ☐ **Smooth-looking but slightly wrinkled outer surface**
- ☐ **Scurfy inside surface**
- ☐ **Outer surface matches colour bar above (top line)**
- ☐ **Inside surface matches colour bar above (bottom line)**

Avg. size across cap:	20–25mm across open funnel
Appearance:	August to November
Habitat:	Near oak and beech
Tip:	Always split them down the middle when cleaning and evict residents
Culinary rating:	10 out of 10. See page 115

Cornucopioides refers to a cornucopia i.e. horn of plenty

Cauliflower Mushroom
Sparassis crispa

This is the mushroom of superlatives. For many people it is the very best of all. It may be a bit chewy but each bite releases a unique culinary sensation. If you fall for it, you'll be a dedicated cauliflower mushroom hunter forever. It resembles a cauliflower or a sponge. Once you learn to recognise its spicy smell, you could identify the cauliflower mushroom blindfolded. And then there is the size: it can grow so big that people simply overlook it. This specimen weighed in at 22.5 lb.

Lobes

Not all specimens grow to giant size. This one here is about the size of two fists. Its cauliflower or sponge-like appearance and the curved lobes are the key identification marks. There is nothing pointed or jagged in the cauliflower mushroom. The colour ranges from creamy white to light brown. If it turns any browner than the specimen here, it has gone off.

Curved lobes

Positive ID Checklist
Cauliflower Mushroom

- ☐ **No gills, pores, tubes or spines**
- ☐ **No stem**
- ☐ **Looks like a cauliflower or sponge**
- ☐ **Lobes**
- ☐ **Matches range of colour bar (above)**

Avg. size:	300mm across but can grow up to a metre
Appearance:	September to October
Habitat:	Mainly near pine or pine stumps
Tip:	Grows on the same spot for many years
Culinary rating:	10 out of 10. See page 115

Crispa means 'frizzy'

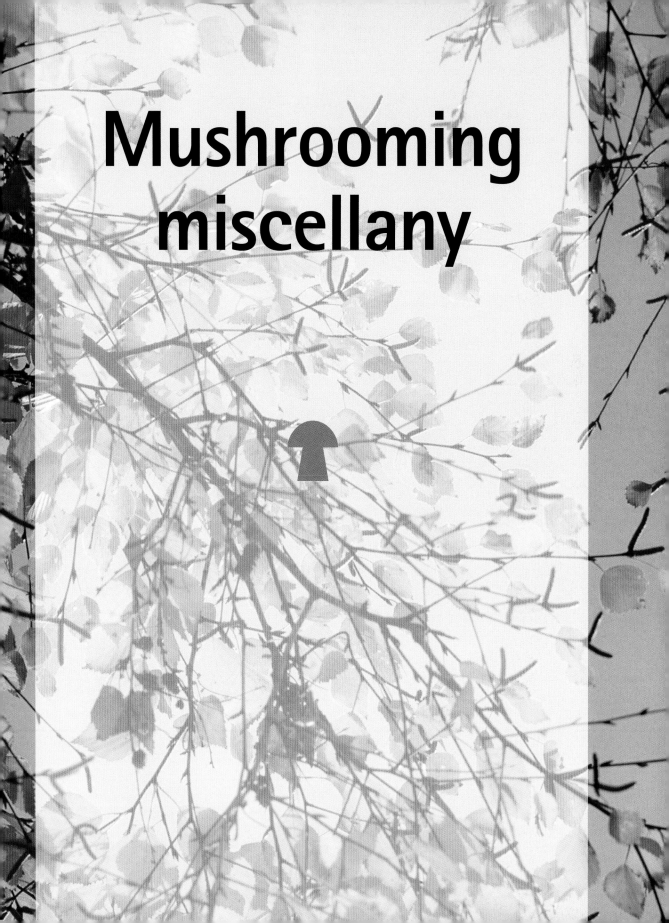

Mushrooming miscellany

The mushrooming season

	J	F	M	A	M	J	J	A	S	O	N	D
Cep							▓	▓	▓	▓	▓	
Red Cracked Bolete						▓	▓	▓	▓	▓	▓	
Dotted Stemmed Bolete							▓	▓	▓	▓		
Larch Bolete						▓	▓	▓	▓	▓	▓	
Bay Bolete						▓	▓	▓	▓	▓	▓	
Birch Bolete							▓	▓	▓	▓	▓	
Chanterelle							▓	▓	▓	▓	▓	
Trumpet Chanterelle							▓	▓	▓	▓	▓	
Hedgehog Fungus								▓	▓	▓	▓	
Puffball							▓	▓	▓	▓		
Horn of Plenty								▓	▓	▓	▓	
Cauliflower Mushroom									▓	▓		

In the northern hemisphere, the classic mushroom months are September and October. The timing and proliferation of mushrooms varies regionally and depends heavily on weather conditions over the whole year. So the dedicated mushroom hunter need not confine himself to a mere two months of pleasure.

Trees and mushrooms

Beech, birch, oak, pine and larch are the most important trees in mushroom-hunting, trees which are easily identifiable by their leaves or bark or both. It is most useful to know these five species of tree because if, for example, you explore a new wood, they will guide you to the mushrooms.

Beech

Especially:
cep, horn of plenty

Oak

Especially:
cep

Birch

Especially:
birch bolete, orange
birch bolete

Pine

Especially:
cauliflower
mushroom

Larch

Especially:
larch bolete

The larch is the only
tree whose needles
change colour in
autumn. You can't
miss it

Always remember

Rule number 1

    Never, never take a mushroom with gills!!!

Rule number 2

    Only take mushrooms with tubes, spines and ridges and the mavericks portrayed in this book

Rule number 3

    Only eat mushrooms which you have clearly identified with ALL the positive ID marks

Rule number 4

    If a mushroom smells rotten, it is rotten and if it feels soggy, it is soggy

Rule number 5

    Never, never eat wild mushrooms raw

Rule number 6

    Look before you cut

Rule number 7

    Mushrooms want to breathe. Do not suffocate them in plastic bags

Rule number 8

    If in doubt, leave it

Handling, storage and cooking

Handling

The first rough cleaning of the mushroom should be done in the wood. Once you're at home you verify your spoils against the positive ID check lists and then – and only then – can you start the fine-cleaning. Do not wet mushrooms to clean them. Brush or wipe them with a cloth. Part of the cleaning process is to check the quality. Evict residents, cut away soft and soggy tubes and cut the remaining mushroom into bite-size pieces.

Storage

Drying

Drying is the classic way to store mushrooms. This method actually intensifies the taste of the mushrooms and they'll keep for years if you follow the procedure correctly. Do not dry anything you wouldn't eat fresh. Drying does not improve the overall quality of your mushrooms. There are various methods of drying mushrooms but there is only one way which guarantees consistent high-quality results and that is the only one I recommend: a dehydrator. Whatever the make, the principle is the same: warm air circulation. The sliced mushrooms are placed on trays and then dried in the dehydrator. Dried mushrooms are best stored in any air-tight container or a sealed plastic bag and then kept in a dark place. Mix all the species except the

cauliflower mushroom. The more species in the mix, the better the taste. The cauliflower mushroom should be dried and stored separately (see page 115). **Do not dry chanterelles.** All other mushrooms in this book are suitable for drying. Dried mushrooms should be crackle-dry and snap when broken.

More on the website: www.mushrooming.co.uk

Freezing

Freezing is the other method. Results improved enormously when home vacuum-packaging machines became available. I recommend only freezing vacuum-packed mushrooms. Frozen mushrooms retain their colour, texture and taste.

Never thaw frozen mushrooms!
Put deep frozen mushrooms in sizzling butter or hot water. Like this they keep their texture.
- Mix all the species except the cauliflower mushroom. Again: the more species in a mix, the better.
- I recommend deep freezing some cep, and horn of plenty, separately. You might want to add just a few of them for a particular dish or use the cep for a tasty starter.

The cauliflower mushroom should always be frozen separately (see page 115).

The chanterelle must be cooked before deep freezing – all other mushrooms in this book can be frozen raw. More on the website: www.mushrooming.co.uk

Drying or freezing?

Either way, use **only perfectly fresh mushrooms.** Drying mushrooms
gives them that deep, strong mushroom taste. The frozen mushroom is
more subtle, but the colours of frozen mushrooms are as bright as on
the day they were picked and this adds considerably to the pleasure of
eating. Dried and frozen mushrooms can be mixed to get the best of
both worlds. More on the website: www.mushrooming.co.uk

Cooking

Famous chefs win awards for stylish cuisine. Simplicity as a rule is not in their repertoire because no stars can be won by doing as little as possible. There are some really attractive mushroom books with some really attractive recipes but my advice is: do not try to emulate the recipes of the famous chefs – you'll never get there anyway. The place to enjoy grande cuisine is in the restaurant.

Do what you can do better than the professionals and do what they can't do and you're in for a feast. Besides, it's much less trouble, expense, and frustration to do it your own way rather than to follow recipes which pre-suppose the infrastructure of a five star establishment.

So where can't the professionals compete with you?

Chervil is a tasty and attractive herb for all mushroom dishes.

1. Freshness

This is not to say that restaurants use old mushrooms. They're just not as fresh as yours.

Your mushrooms have the shorter way from the wood to your kitchen. As a rule the restaurants' mushrooms come from a market and some of those mushrooms on the market have travelled a long way. Some of them half way round the world.

2. Sourcing

You know where your mushrooms came from, whereas the chef in the restaurant, as a rule, knows only that it is the type of mushroom he wants. You know the very wood from which you picked them, and this is important because, for example, a cep can taste differently from one wood to another.

3. Quality

You know exactly where your mushrooms come from, and therefore you know their quality. In other words, you can be sure, for example, that your mushrooms grew in a non-polluted habitat or a dog-free zone.

Garnishing with finely chopped vegetables makes your mushroom dish a feast for the eyes.

4. Freedom

You are at liberty to vary the mushrooms that go into your dish and to change ingredients. In top restaurants, recipes are more precise and designed to be produced time and again. Your mushroom feast, on the other hand, can be unique each time.

5. Soul

There is a satisfaction in picking your own wild mushrooms and cooking them yourself that nothing can match.

Mushrooms are not garnish

The mushrooms in this book are of culinary value in their own right and should be treated accordingly. Treat a wild mushroom with the same culinary respect as you would a wild salmon.

Olive oil and mushrooms

Most contemporary mushroom recipe books recommend olive oil for cooking mushrooms, but if you really want to draw out all the subtle flavours of your mushrooms and realize their full culinary potential, then olive oil is, generally, not a good idea. Salt-free butter brings out the best in your mushrooms.

Chives are the classic garnish for mushrooms.

Kills all known germs

There is a potential but very low risk of catching something nasty from a mushroom. To reduce that risk to zero, do not eat raw mushrooms and in the cooking process, increase the heat at one stage so that the dish either boils for a couple of seconds or sizzles in the butter. For that brief moment, turn the mushrooms in the pan so that they're exposed to the heat on all sides.

Curly or flat-leafed parsley underline the mushroom taste and add aesthetic appeal. Sprinkle on raw just before serving.

Special Cases

Chanterelle

The chanterelle must not be dried because it goes chewy. It must not be frozen without prior cooking because it will turn bitter.

Horn of Plenty

Some people like it on its own. Others use it only as a spice to add to a mix of mushrooms. In order to find out what you like best, dry and freeze separately.

Cauliflower mushroom

The cauliflower mushroom is also very distinct in taste and perhaps best on its own. Dry or deep freeze separately.

More on the website: www.mushrooming.co.uk

Basic preparation for fresh or frozen mushrooms

There's a lot of leeway in these basic preparations. The amounts stated can vary considerably and you'll still get an excellent result. And the beauty of it is that you can't overdo mushrooms. The key to culinary success is the quality of the mushrooms.

Serves 4

What you need

Essential:	300–600 g fresh or frozen mushrooms
	800 ml – 1 litre water
	100–200 ml white wine
	1 teaspoon vegetable extract
	1 shallot or small onion, chopped
	100–200 ml cream
	10–20 g chives or parsley
Optional:	A mix of finely chopped vegetables e.g. carrot, courgette and celery: approx. 70 g
	10–20 g chervil

What you do

1. Put water, white wine, vegetable extract and shallot into a pan

2. Do not thaw frozen mushrooms. Add frozen or fresh
    mushrooms and bring to the boil

3. Reduce heat and simmer until approx $2/3$ of liquid has evaporated

4. Add cream

5. Simmer again until approx. half the liquid has evaporated. Stir occasionally.
    If you feel there's too much liquid, simmer until it reduces still further.
    The less liquid, the more intense the taste and vice versa. Add water or cream
    to taste.

6. Add salt to taste

7. You now have a wonderful mushroom sauce which you can serve with
    meat (chops, steak etc) or on its own with pasta or rice.
    Sprinkle with chives, parsley or chervil and the finely chopped vegetables

Basic preparation of dried mushrooms

Serves 4

What you need

Essential: 30–60 g dried mushrooms

1 litre lukewarm water

1 shallot or small onion chopped

200 ml dry white wine

1 teaspoon vegetable extract

150–200 ml cream

10–20 g chives or parsley

Optional: A mix of finely chopped vegetables e.g. carrot, courgette

and celery: approx. 70 g

10–20 g chervil

What you do

1. Take the dried mushrooms and put in a bowl or pitcher. Add 1 litre of lukewarm water. Soak for $1^{1}/_{2}$ hours (until the mushrooms float in brown liquid)
2. Put wine, shallot, vegetable extract, mushrooms and the brown liquid into a pan
3. Bring to the boil for 10 seconds Reduce heat and simmer until $^{2}/_{3}$ of the liquid has evaporated

4. Add the cream

5. Simmer until approx. half the liquid has evaporated. Stir occasionally. If there is too much liquid, simmer until further reduced. The less liquid the more intense the flavour, and vice versa
Add water or cream to taste

6. Add salt to taste

7. You now have a wonderful mushroom sauce which you can serve with meat (chops, steak etc.) or on its own with pasta or rice. Sprinkle with chives, parsley or chervil and the finely chopped vegetables

For more about these basic preparations and on cooking mushrooms, visit the website www.mushrooming.co.uk

Beyond the stove

No summer or winter woodland walk will ever be the same again once you become aware of the amazing universe of the forest floor, which in terms of colour and life is a match for any coral reef. And the forest floor is right at your feet, so to speak, or at least not far from your door.

When in autumn you walk through a beech wood and marvel at the intensity and variety of the colours, think for a moment about those leaves.

There are about 3 to 4 metric tons of leaves to one hectare of beech wood. After their job is done on the branches, they fall to the ground. If they did not decompose we would soon be swimming through a sea of leaves. Likewise, unrotted fallen branches would in time pile up as insurmountable obstacles. A leaf falls to the ground, inspiring on its way a poet who happens to be passing by: but on a more practical level, bacteria are the first organisms to get busy.

Shortly afterwards, it is fungi, algae and protozoans which play their part in the work of decomposition.

Soon, millions of organisms and little animals are at work on that single leaf. In due course the leaf is fully decomposed, its constituent parts recycled back into the forest soil, keeping it fertile by providing the essential substances for all the plants in the wood.

The vital role of mushrooms

Fungi are key players in maintaining tree growth and health. The reason the birch bolete is always found near birch trees, and the larch bolete always near larch trees, is that these pairs live in a symbiotic relationship. They need each other.

The mycelium of the birch bolete and the fine root-ends of the birch tree link up and exchange substances. There is a lot of chemistry going on, with a net result of mutual benefit. There are intricacies and complexities in all matters fungi and there are, so to speak, vast uncharted areas on the fungal map. However, even the most half-hearted mushroom-hunter will soon become aware of the all-encompassing interrelations in the wood. Mushrooming makes you see and appreciate the woodland differently.

There is a practical point to these impressions which will help you in your mushrooming.

The similarity of patterning between the trunk of the birch tree and the stalk of the birch bolete is there for all to see. The similarity in colour between the larch needles (once they change colour in autumn) and the larch bolete seems obvious. These pointers can all act as nature's clues and reminders for the mushroom forager. But why is this so? Whatever the scientific answer, if indeed there is one, this

similarity illustrates beautifully the inter-connected nature or, if you prefer it, the mutual dependence, of life in the wood.

Perhaps even more intriguing is the similarity between the pine bark and the cauliflower mushroom, which grows near pine trees. It could be a co-incidence or it could be a complex pattern at work. Either way, the cauliflower mushroom is utterly delicious – but if you mull over a conundrum like this, doesn't it add interest and pleasure to mushroom hunting?

But I still want more advice on the secrets of successful mushrooming.

Mushroom hunting and the world of fungi have more than their fair share of mysterious lore, imponderables and surprises. Take that inexplicable instinct for the right spot to find mushrooms, for example. The experienced mushroomer knows his favourite haunts and whenever conditions are right, the mushrooms seem to call him. The dedicated mushroom hunter doesn't have to make a conscious effort to memorise the perfect weather conditions for a particular species. Nor does he have to keep a log on the wind direction. Over the years, he just knows that on the right day he has to go to spot X. As vague as that sounds, the mushrooming 'instinct' may well have a rational explanation, but it needn't be a conscious one.

No exact science to mushrooming-hunting, then?

True, if you meet gnomes, pixies, fairies, elves or goblins in the woods, your rationality will be doubted. But when fingers of fog creep eerily through the lonely wood, mythical creatures don't seem far away. When out mushrooming in the twilight, you can easily understand how our forebears believed there were strange goings-on in the woods. Perhaps there

were: and perhaps our modern powers of perception are just that much weaker than they used to be. The cold light of reason may have evicted all those colourful beings from the woods and now nobody is quite sure where they are any more.

But they did leave their mark. The last bastion of mysticism is the fly agaric (left) which to this day has the power to fire the imagination. No decent fairy tale illustration is complete without the fly agaric. If the cep is the king of mushrooms, the fly agaric must be the queen. And as always with mushrooms, the mystical mixes with the scientific.

Fly agarics are useful indicators: where they are, there are often ceps nearby. Fly agarics wave and shout 'Over here! Over here there are beautiful ceps!' The king is always near the queen.

Yet another mingling of fact and fiction: the fly agaric got its name from its surprising powers: it is a natural insecticide. Pieces of it are put in milk to attract flies. The flies then get stoned and die. In fact, the hallucinogenic properties of the fly agaric have inspired some mind-boggling theories and experiences.

Shamans, or holy priests, reportedly used the hallucinogenic fly agaric to make contact with the gods, while lesser mortals joined in the ritual by drinking the urine of the shaman. This would have been little more than water with the hallucinogenic substances still active in it, because, before the ceremony, the shaman had to fast for several days before ingesting the fly agaric.

The phrase 'to go berserk' refers to the Berserkers (Viking warriors) who went fearlessly into battle and were reported to fight 'like mad dogs and wolves'. This is said to be the fly agaric's work.

It surely now comes as no surprise that Santa Claus is also linked to the fly agaric. After all, there are the same distinctive colours: and there he is in his reindeer-powered sledge, flying all over the world, filling stockings and involuntarily cleaning chimneys. Only a fully-blown shamanic fly agaric ritual could take Saint Nicholas and come up with a tale like that!

These are just a few of the theories and ideas linked to the fly agaric. Fly agarics are also supposed to bring good luck, and in central and northern Europe they remain a popular emblem in advertising, on stamps and especially on Christmas and New Year cards. Luck is a fitting theme with which to conclude this book. Don't trust your luck when identifying mushrooms. Follow the instructions in this book and enjoy mushrooming without fear.